Winning at Work

HOW TO BE A GREAT EMPLOYEE

Walt Mulvey

Published by
Hara Publishing
P.O. Box 19732
Seattle, WA 98109

ISBN: 1-883697-45-X
Library of Congress Number: 95-076235

Preface

*I*f you are an employee, this book is written for you. Over the last 30 years I have been an entrepreneur, an employee and a boss. During that time I have experienced hundreds upon hundred of "work related" situations which were new to me, and, for whatever reason, made an impression upon me.

During this period (especially the last 10 years), I have had this little man in the back of my brain causing me lots of turmoil. This little guy has kept saying, "Write a book to help employees become better employees. You've done a few things right and a few wrong. Share it with the world."

Then I would respond to that little guy, "I have too much to do as it is. You don't know what it takes to write, publish, and sell a book." This little guy kept getting bigger and bigger, and he was persistent. He finally got my attention when he said, "Do you know how many books have been written to help managers become better managers?" I responded, "Thousands." He said, "How many books have been written to help employees become better employees?" I said, "I don't think I have ever seen one." He got me—and I started writing my dream.

As Chapter 9 of this book states, dreams do come true. And they can for you as a *Great Employee*. If it is your desire to fulfill your goals as an employee, you will enjoy and benefit from this book. If you are an employee now (that means you're not a boss) but you desire to move into management, this book will help you now and in the future as a "boss."

You will find that each chapter contains a variety of actual experiences which relate to the chapter's theme. Nine of the chapters will also give you the *Great Employees' 10 Tips* which will help you improve your performance in everything from your attitude to your communication skills.

And always remember, this book was written for one reason only, so that you can benefit from my experience and my fellow employees' experiences. This book is not written by a Ph.D. Don't look for any theory. This book is a basic, simple, little book, written from the human perspective.

I wish I had room to thank all of those who have helped me with this dream. I would especially like to thank my family and my wonderful wife, C.J. When you read this book and say to yourself, "I used to work with him." then you probably contributed to it in some fashion.

Good luck, wherever you career takes you. I truly hope the next 100 pages will help you in some small way become a *Great Employee*!

Contents

"I don't need to be Tom Cruise. I just need to work forever."
Jodie Foster

1
Why Work?

*T*he response to this question seems obvious—"for money." And the response does make sense, "I've got bills to pay." "I want to buy a new car." "I gotta eat." "I need a place to live." So the first and basic response revolves around basic needs: food, water, and shelter. It's called survival. That's just the beginning. You work for many more reasons than the money. After all, money can't buy everything.

There has got to be a reason why you wake up to that awful alarm clock at 5:30, only to put it on snooze for another 15 minutes. "Why do I have to get up so early? I'll just sleep a little more." Then it hits you: rent, bills, food, Friday nights, savings, car payment. So you drag out of bed, hit the coffee maker, and head for the shower.

Now you have made it to the car. You are sitting in traffic changing the radio stations, cursing the guy next to you for cutting you off earlier. The light changes and you're on your way—almost. The lady in front of you hits her brakes, you are now skidding and coffee is spilling! Why do you have to go through this five times a week? For the answer, go back to the first paragraph.

Now you have made it to the office. "Oh, I hope time flies by today. Wait, that pile of papers is exactly where I left it last night. Where's the work fairy to take them away?" Darn, you forgot that meeting with your boss. Now the phone starts ringing. Are we having fun yet?

Or maybe you have just made it to the store or the fast-food restaurant. "Why are the customers so backed up? Everybody seems to be just standing around. Am I the only one who works around here? I gotta find another job! Why doesn't the boss say something?"

With some luck, you make it through the day, and now it's time to fight the traffic in reverse. "Those busses, why do I always get stuck behind them? Uh oh, what's for dinner? Was I suppose to get something or was she?" Luckily, she was and did. Now some time for the kids, maybe a little TV, and then off to bed, only to face tomorrow. Don't worry, it's got to be a better day.

Does all this sound familiar? Maybe not for you, but surely for many of your co-workers. Well, for whomever, we are going to change all that. In the next 98 pages, we'll provide you with ways to become a *Great Employee.* But these are only the tools of the trade—you have to pick them up and use them. You must commit yourself to the task. With this book, you can change your entire outlook on work. Work can bring you more reward than you thought possible.

The *Great Employees'* Definition of Work: Read Chapters 1 through 10.

Let's get rid of the ugly stuff first. The world owes you nothing. You must make your place in the world. Don't even think about griping. If you do, go directly to Chapter 4. You are not a victim. The world is going to treat you with the same respect and attitude as you project.

Okay, now for some fun stuff. Stop for a minute, go to a mirror, and look at yourself. You are a beautiful person. You are the only person in this entire world who is just like you. You have your whole life ahead of you, no matter if you are 15 or 80. You have a chance to make your mark. How exciting!

Starting today, look at yourself and see someone who can be courageous, venturesome, loyal, generous, kind, considerate, flexible, thoughtful, energetic and happy. Put misfortune and frustration behind you forever.

By reading **Winning at Work,** you will quickly learn several techniques to use daily. These **Tips** will help you with the many challenges and frustrations you experience every day. This book is based on the experiences of many people, which are condensed into 100 pages to give you an advantage at work—an advantage to become a **Great Employee**.

Do you remember your first job? For the women, it was probably babysitting. For the men, it could have been mowing lawns or shoveling snow. That's when it all started. Your life changed at that point. You learned that you could do something for someone and in return you would receive *something* for doing it.

What was that something? I didn't say you were paid for it. I said you received *something* for it, which may have been the thrill of a first job. It could have been your pride about the way you shoveled that sidewalk. "Much better than Bobby's job across the street." That first babysitting job had to be a thrill. It was almost like being a mommy. The way you read that bedtime story—it had to give you a fantastic feeling. On top of that, you got paid for it.

I shoveled snow in Spokane, Washington, and Rapid City, South Dakota. Even then, I was expansion-oriented. My routine was, "Can I shovel your sidewalk. I don't charge anything. Just pay me what you think it is worth." Then, of course, I would shiver and make sure they saw my wet mittens. I got 'em every time. They always paid me more than the going rate which, in those days, was twenty-five cents.

And, of course, you had something you wanted to do with the money. Toys, clothes, movies, presents for Christmas, birthdays. Mostly material things. That's why you worked— kind of like the first paragraph of this chapter. But in time those needs and desires derived from work expanded to include much more than money.

So let's take another look at the question, "Why Work?" It's not just for the dough. You can get so much more from working. Think about the gratification you get when you do a task that was just a little more *difficult* than you expected. As a merchandising buyer, I remember how thrilled I was with my first buy when I beat the price down by about 10%. I didn't think I could ever negotiate a better price, especially as a rookie buyer. The disappointing fact was that the merchandise I bought hung around the store for years. But that was okay. I learned that the merchandise was not as saleable as I thought, and that was why I "got such a great deal." The next time a vendor offered a quick discount, I walked.

Think for a minute about the contribution you can make at work. It doesn't matter how menial the job is. I have seen more employees become successful because they took a simple "grunt job" and made names for themselves by doing something special with it. You must have a cookie lady or guy who comes through the office to sell muffins or cookies. Well, we had this guy who was so happy and positive we waited more for him than the cookies. If he missed a day, we were in a frump. He had special way about him. We will talk more about attitude in Chapter 4.

What about friends at work? Don't they become a part of your life just as you job does? You learn about their families, their goals, their opinions. People need people, and work provides an excellent source for personal contact. Be friendly—just don't get too personal with those at work. It can make for difficult times down the road.

Work also provides an opportunity to learn. I don't think there is another platform in your life that provides for as much opportunity to learn as does work. And the more you learn, the better you perform. The better you perform, the more satisfaction, contribution, and productivity you are able to enjoy.

Now, to be a **_Great Employee_**, you must enjoy your work. Do not feel badly if a job is not right for you. Do not get locked into it. You must do something you enjoy. Too many employees are going through the motions. They do their job, but, on a scale of ten, they are about a six. If you are performing at a level less than eight, go find another job. But before you do, make sure you have given the job your all.

Have you tried to make the job rewarding by adding a new twist to it? What could you change about the job to make it enjoyable for you. Don't get me wrong. Work is not like play. It is not something that you can do 40 or 50 hours a week and have fun all the time you're doing it. But the more you enjoy your work the easier it becomes.

It's all up to you. Ever hear the story about the man walking down a street and seeing several masons laying bricks? The man approached one of the masons and asked, "What are you doing?" The mason replied, "Can't you see, I am laying bricks." The man walked a little further and asked another mason what he was doing. That mason replied, "I am building a church. No, not just a church. This church will be a masterpiece where people will come to rejoice in God. Parents will bring their children here for baptism. Vows will be exchanged here. Couples will unite into one. Friends will come here to pay their last respects. This is a grand palace I am building." Wow! What a difference in perspective.

As you read this book (I hope you go on to the next chapters) you will note that every chapter ends with the *Great Employees' 10 Tips*. These tips are to help you learn from the experiences of many people over many years. I hope you will get as much benefit from them as I have had satisfaction writing them. Good luck and good fortune.

Let's launch into the *Great Employees' 10 Tips for:*

Winning at Work

1. *You gotta have goals to be a success.* Without goals you don't know where you are because you have nothing to measure yourself against. Both personal and career goals are important. It takes guts to write down your goals because of fear of failure. But goals can change. The important thing is to strive to accomplish your goals. That will bring you more success than those employees without them. "I guarantee it."

2. *Great Employees don't have jobs, they have careers.* There is so much more to you than "just a job." If you find yourself thinking that way, it is time to move on to something that is not "just a job," but rather, "just about the greatest thing that ever happened to me." But make absolutely sure you have done everything to make that job into something rewarding. Remember that a career is a lifetime. Your career will probably take many twists and turns that you can't see at this point. Make sure your goals and your career are tied together.

3. *There is nothing more important to your success than your attitude.* Most people let their attitude control them. This book will not only teach you how to control your attitude but also how to develop a positive, get-it-done attitude. I have seen more **Great Employees** achieve success because of their positive attitudes than any other trait. We are going to work on attitude a lot in this book. You will see it in every chapter.

4. *Great Employees work extra hard on communicating.* We do so much talking and listening at work, but as important as it is, we don't spend enough time developing our communication skills. Few of us work on expanding our vocabularies. Can you list three important factors in listening? What do you do when you listen? How far in advance do you think about what you are going to say? Do you realize what your body is doing when you talk? Think about your forehead, your eyebrows, your head, your hands. They all are part of communicating. Do you understand what I said? Do you understand what I meant? Two totally different questions.

5. *Great Employees are boss boosters.* They have a special understanding of their bosses' needs. They recognize that they may not have been trained in management and could use some help. As your boss goes, you go. A successful boss has successful employees. *Great Employees* work to make their bosses look great!

6. *The Great Employee knows that any business, association, or organization has customers.* But the *Great Employee* focuses not only on the external customer, but also the internal customer. The internal customer is any other employee or department in the organization. The *Great Employee* strives to service those employees or departments as if they were external customers. It is amazing how many customers the *Great Employee* amasses. That is part of his or her success.

7. *The Great Employee knows that the folks "at the top" have certain opinions of what makes a Great Employee.* They know that the important traits may vary, but they usually include characteristics such as loyalty, hard work, discipline, commitment, energy, positive attitude, honesty, resourcefulness and responsiveness. So they strive to develop those traits as they work. You will be amazed how much the bosses and the *Great Employee* look alike.

8. *The Great Employee knows what it takes to be a Great Employee and strives to do those things.* They know they can't be *Great Employees* without being loyal to their employers and their bosses. They know that success is going to take lots of hard work. They know they will have to go the extra mile, and to do that they must be disciplined to hang in there. They know what management wants. But they also know that those traits are what they would want and will want, when and if they choose to become managers. However there are tons of **Great Employees** who prefer to be employees and do not want to join the ranks of management. *And that's okay!*

9. **Great Employees are what this country is built on.** It is not management. Sure, the leaders have their place in this world, but they have to have somebody to lead. And if they can't lead **Great Employees,** they can't be Great Leaders. That is why Great Leaders are always looking for **Great Employees**. The two have a lot in common. They speak the same language.

10. **Great Employees are not born that way.** Their upbringing may help them with their work ethic and work habits. But anyone can become a **Great Employee** regardless of the family, education, or intelligence. You may be a **Great Employee** now. If you are not, I hope this book will help you become one. Anyone can do it. Only the great choose to do it.

"Get in my way when I really want to accomplish something, I can be a mean mother."
— Dick Clark

2

Goals—The Only Way to Score

Goals! Everybody should have them, but few of us do. Not many of us really take the time to develop our own set of personal goals. Most of us actually spend more time planning our annual vacation than our career goals. There are obvious reasons for this. Many of us feel we have little control over our own destiny. And we may lack imagination when it comes to goal setting. But the really big reason we don't spend much time planning our future is *the fear of failure.* We don't want to commit ourselves to something we may not accomplish. By overcoming this fear with courage and dedication we can achieve the goals that will bring health, wealth, and happiness. Dale Carnegie said, "You can't get anywhere in this world without wanting to do something."

**The *Great Employees'* Definition of Goals:
If you ain't where you're at when you're there,
you're nowhere.**

Now remember, this book is written for the employee. It is not written for the manager. But you would be amazed at how many managers and companies *"do not know where they are at when they are there."* I worked recently with a retailer who has 30 stores. Every morning, like most retailers, the management group would come in and look at the previous day's sales results and make statements like, "Store 12 had a great day." "Store 7 really sucked." "Not that great of a day—compared to last year,"—in other words, "same store sales."

Retailers are really into this "same store sales" stuff. That means how well each store did yesterday as compared to the same day last year.

What is missing? What is wrong with this picture? Lots! These guys *did not know where they were at when they were there*—so guess what—*they were nowhere.* Now the reason they were nowhere is because they were measuring their performance against last year's sales or maybe sales from the day before. The big fallacy in this is that they *are not* measuring their performance against *goals*.

The concept of same store sales has nothing to do with same store *goals*. Perhaps a store has been hit with two new competitors. Perhaps a store has lost two key employees. There are a multitude of reasons a store may not be doing well against last year's numbers. But, given the circumstances, the store may be doing well measured against its goals—goals which have been based on a number of factors that are both external and internal.

Now back to you, the employee. You will be a *Great Employee* once you learn how to set goals, and how to use those goals to measure your performance. Once properly used, goal-setting will become a passion—a passion to *achieve.*

Goals can be career-oriented, money-oriented, personally-oriented, or just "anything-oriented." Hey, we're talking about you here. Attention! We are talking about making you a *Great Employee,* and to be a *Great Employee* you gotta have goals. We are going to take care of that in this chapter. *You are too good not to have goals.* Someday one of you will be famous and *I* want you to think it was due in part to my book. (Please call if that occurs.)

A survey of graduates of Yale University was done to determine their success rate. The initial phase of the study found that only one in ten graduates had set specific goals. We are talking Yale here, folks. I suppose more than 10% knew what they wanted to do in life. But only 10% had actually taken the time to establish goals for themselves.

Twenty years later, a follow-up study was done. It showed that the goal setters were more productive, better off financially and had a higher level of satisfaction with their lots in life. Surprising to any of us? No! Why? Because those with the higher success levels *knew where they were at when they were there, so they were somewhere.*

Several years ago I had the opportunity to meet Bill Medley who was one of the Righteous Brothers, a famous rock group in the mid-60s. These guys were great. They had everything going, one hit after another. Then suddenly, they broke up. I loved rock-and-roll and at the time I was shattered. No more Righteous Brothers. That's un-American. Medley still sings and has had a few hits in the last several years, but nothing to match his success with the Righteous Brothers.

When he appeared in Portland, Oregon, in 1985, I posed as a reporter to get into his dressing room. Thank God for my fake press pass. Man, I was on cloud nine. Drinking a beer with Bill Medley. Out of the blue, Bill Medley says, "Want to grab a taco with me?" I had to say yes. But since he thinks I'm a reporter I gotta ask him lots of questions at dinner.

Here is the point to this whole story: I asked him why he and Bobby Hatfield broke up. His answer made me choke on my enchilada. He said, "We didn't know who we were." In 1966, these guys were 23 or 24 years old, had worked for six or seven years to get to where they were and did not realize how popular they were. In other words, *they did not know where they were at when they were there, so they were nowhere.*

I learn slow! In 10 years as a banker, I thought that I set goals at work every year. It took me that long to realize that the only time I set goals was during the annual review I took part in at my job. But that review process was usually not the best. Why? Typically the annual review was done in tandem with the annual raise. And truthfully, I was more focused on the annual raise than the annual review.

Many companies have altered the process, so now the raise and review are performed at separate times. That doesn't work very well either, because then they have a hard time tying the raise to the performance.

There I was, setting my goals at a time when I was more focused on a raise—with the help of my boss who, in some of my jobs, was not well trained to assist. That was why I said to myself, "It is time to take charge." Then I accepted the responsibility for setting my goals. By doing so, I gained more control of my life. It was at that point that my "life" began to really expand. I looked at things differently, I woke up to more of the things and people around me. I gained more purpose to my life. *I began to know where I was at when I was there.*

Now, to be a *Great Employee* you must feel good about yourself. To feel good about yourself you must be able to evaluate your level of success, be it personal or professional. To evaluate your success—you guessed it—*you gotta know where you're at when your there, or you're nowhere.*

Before we get into the goal setting process, let's quickly talk about two important things. *One is a priority and the other is a goal.* Think of a priority as a big goal. Then the goals are those items that you need to do to accomplish your priority. Make sense?

Maybe developing a closer relationship with your daughter is a priority. Then you need to establish some things to do (goals) to accomplish the priority of knowing your daughter better. Maybe a priority is a job change. What are four goals which would achieve the job change?

We are now to the point where we review the ***Great Employees' 10 Tips On:***

Setting Priorities and Goals

1. *Take an inventory of yourself.* Who am I? What do I stand for? What are my likes and dislikes? What kind of work do I enjoy? What kind of play do I enjoy? What kind of people do I enjoy? Look around. Where am I today? Where do I live? Who are my friends? Where do I work? What is my current income?

2. *Ask someone you are close to for help in analyzing who you are.* Now that is a tough suggestion. Why? You may not want to hear what they have to say. But a close friend's or spouse's input will prove invaluable.

3. *Write out your priorities, both personal and for your career.* Make sure you are in the right state of mind to do this. After a tough day at work is not one of those times. Choose some quiet time when you are completely relaxed, with nothing around to break your concentration.

Establishing priorities will bring more direction and organization into your life. They provide the meaning and purpose to support your goals. By achieving your goals, one at a time, you will also accomplish your priorities.

4. ***Think of yourself as a box divided into four smaller boxes.*** The four boxes contain your priorities. Now divide each of the boxes into four smaller boxes. Those represent your goals. As each goal is reached, you will be that much closer to fulfilling your priority. *(See chart on next page.)*

5. ***Establish some goals for yourself.*** Set goals that are clear, challenging, and attainable. Take a look at your first priority. Is it personal or work-related? If work-related, identify at least four goals you want to accomplish on the job during the next year. Remember, each of these four goals fills one of the four boxes and will help you accomplish your priorities.

6. ***Outline how you are going to accomplish each goal.*** Identify the barriers which exist that prevent you from accomplishing your goal. Then identify ways to overcome the barriers. And be sure to set a timetable. Some goals may take three months while others will take the full year.

Name: _____ *Date:* _____

Priority: _____

Goal: _____
_____

Goal: _____
_____

Goal: _____
_____

Goal: _____
_____

Priority: _____

Goal: _____
_____

Goal: _____
_____

Goal: _____
_____

Goal: _____
_____

Priority: _____

Goal: _____
_____

Goal: _____
_____

Goal: _____
_____

Goal: _____
_____

Priority: _____

Goal: _____
_____

Goal: _____
_____

Goal: _____
_____

Goal: _____
_____

7. *Review your goals at least monthly.* Monitor your progress and be honest. When setting your goals, be sure to include some ways to measure your performance. A priority to achieve a higher level of income can be easily monitored. However, does your plan to achieve that level of income have four goals that you must achieve during the coming year?

8. *Think about your priorities and goals daily.* That doesn't mean you have to pull out your priority-setting sheet daily, but don't lose sight of where you want to be and what you have to do to get there. You do need to review the sheet monthly, however. Some people keep the sheet at work, some by the bed, some on the refrigerator.

Do you see now how this process will give you more direction and organization to your life? *It's great!*

9. ***When you reach a goal, celebrate!!*** You have accomplished a task you set out to do. All of us need to celebrate more. That's our reinforcement. You gotta reinforce yourself. If you don't recognize yourself and applaud yourself, then probably nobody else is going to do it for you. ***So, when you know where you're at when you're there, and it's the goal—CELEBRATE.***

10. ***The last important point in setting and striving to achieve goals is to recognize that they can be changed.*** Once you have set out to achieve your goals, you will, in all likelihood, find barriers that you did not anticipate. So take the time to adjust the plan. Larry Wilson, of the Pecos River Learning Institute says, *"It is not the plan that is important. It is the planning process which achieves success."* Be flexible, but do not allow yourself to abort a goal because it appears too difficult at one time or another. You must have the courage to stick to the task of *achieving*. It will be a struggle, no doubt, but, once you learn to discipline, motivate, and measure yourself, you will be on your way toward becoming a ***Great Employee***.

"I do not try to dance better than anyone else. I only try to dance better than myself."
— Mikhail Baryshnikov

3

Whose Career Is This?

Wouldn't it be great if we knew in advance the various twists that our careers would take? We are talking about a period of time of up to fifty years. And yet we have no idea what these years will bring. Even so, we are out there every day of our lives, working on our careers. Not a day goes by that we don't think about our careers. This is why we need a chapter on career planning. We talked about the importance of goal setting earlier. Career planning is different. By combining goal setting with career planning, you will take another step toward becoming a *Great Employee*.

Career planning is much more complex and longer term than goal setting. Career planning requires much more balancing of wants, needs, changes, requirements and challenges. You no doubt have met someone who has not progressed through the ranks as far or as quickly as you thought they would. In most cases, those people made some "career mistakes."

The problem with career decisions and career mistakes is that they take so long to surface. The same with career successes. Let's go back to 1969. A friend of mine had just graduated from college. He interviewed with many companies and narrowed his choice to two employers—First Interstate Bank and Coopers & Lybrand, then the largest accounting firm in the country. The accounting firm paid fifty dollars more a month. Guess which job he took? Right, he went with Coopers and Lybrand. To make a short story long, he went from there to another company, where by 1980 he had amassed a good-sized fortune. He has been "retired" since then and spends his time between homes in Hawaii, Palm Desert and who knows where else. All this for fifty dollars. Makes this ten dollar book look pretty good.

Okay, I shouldn't have even told you about my buddy. Actually, he's not my buddy anymore—he has too much money. But, anyway, he is one in a million. Most careers span a much longer time period. And you know what? He will probably be back for another career before it's all over.

The *Great Employees'* Definition of Career: Your Lifelong Opportunity.

You see, careers are for life. That's a long time if you live to be one hundred and have your name announced on the Today Show by Willard Scott. Jobs come and go. Careers don't. Jobs pay dollars, careers pay dividends. Think about it like this: Jobs may be short term, careers are long term. You know, like a career criminal versus one robbery. Not a good example—but it will stick.

Reminds me of another friend. During college he ran out of money during his senior year. To supplement his funding, he drove fifty miles and robbed a gas station. The whole project took two hours of planning and one hour of executing.

He "generated" enough money to finish college. Then he went on to a post graduate degree—in law. Now he practices law in a state that only I know. Another bad example. But the robbery was certainly a career decision that he, and now you, along with me, will never forget.

Are you getting the feel for career decisions? I am not going to bore you with my career decisions, although they have been somewhat interesting. The biggest and best was the one to write this book. I mean, how many people do you know who would walk from a $250,000-a-year job to write a 100 page book, with no editor and no publisher? Am I nuts?

But, my friend, if you bought my book, that's what careers are made of. Two years from now, I will either look back and say to myself, my wife, and the kids, "Boy did I screw up!" or, "Am I a genius or what?"

Your career will have its ups and downs. It ain't going to be all success. There will be failure too. Do not forget that. Never, never forget that. We will return to that thought. Okay, so now you know that careers are long term, and they depend on decisive decisions. There are two more ingredients— bounce and luck. You know, like, "How'd they do that?" Some people with bounce and luck are: Sonny Bono, John Travolta,

Tina Turner, Richard Nixon, and the big one, Elvis. God, I hope he reads this book!

It is important that you understand that careers depend on a number of elements working in a dynamic environment. So here are the **Great Employees' 10 Tips On:**

What Makes Your Career

1. *You.* That is a sentence, I don't care what the editors say. Keep those eyes open. Be ready to pounce. Develop a nose for smelling success. Remember, the key to your success is you. *Great Employees* know that they are responsible for their success.

2. *Work.* We talk about the importance of hard and smart work throughout this book. Abraham Lincoln said something like, "Work hard, practice, practice, practice, because someday you will be called upon to show the skills of your practice." *Great Employees* know that their success depends on their level of commitment to work. They work harder than other employees. They sacrifice many pleasures to make sure their performance is at maximum. They just simply go further than the nine-to-five employee.

3. *People.* I hate to inject this one, but you gotta know it by now if you didn't know it before. *People skills* are extremely important in your career. There is absolutely no substitute. I have seen more people go further than imaginable with simply their people skills. And they deserve it! There is nothing more important than people skills to help you be accepted in an organization. You might want to refer to Chapter 5 on communication. Some of that information can help you with your these skills. There are hundreds of books on people skills. You also might want to refer to Chapter 6 on boosting your boss. Look at the *10 Tips* for working with your boss. Apply those tips to your fellow employees as well.

4. *Timing.* "She was in the right place at the right time." It happens. But think about this one. How do **Great Employees** seem to be in the right place? If you are in the right place, eventually the time is going to come, although it will probably take longer than you expect. Just make sure you get to the right place.

5. *Ability.* Forget it! Everyone has ability. The **Great Employee** knows that it is necessary to harness his or her ability and convert it into performance. If you are not maximizing your performance you may simply be lacking motivation. Here is a story a friend told me about his stepson. This child was a real discipline problem. Bad stuff. Example: he set a field on fire. My friend and his wife started working with their son to help him appreciate himself. One year later, he was still misbehaving. Now, don't ask me why, but his teachers took him out of the third grade and put him with the fifth graders. And they said, "If you do well, we will put you back with your friends in the third grade." Now, this kid is my kind of guy. He said, "I wanna stay here with the fifth graders." So the teachers say, "Okay, do well and you can stay with the fifth graders." This last grading period, the kid was on the honor roll. Here's to you Dirk, and to your folks, Rose Ann and Chuck. Congratulations!

6. *Vision.* You need to look way out there into the future. Remember my buddy at Coopers and Lybrand. He didn't just choose them for fifty bucks. He saw more opportunity with an accounting firm than a bank *for him.* **Great Employees** make an effort to look into the future to guide their success. A buddy of mine started a movie rental business ten years ago. He went to the Consumer Electronics Show in Chicago that year and saw all these people trying to sell VCRs. He said to himself, "What is John Q. America going to put in those things?" Answer: Movies. Question: Where are they gonna get the movies? Answer: From me at $3 a day. Yes! Today his company is worth millions. And he started it with $17. Not a bad vision!

7. **Luck.** *The harder I work, the luckier I get.* I have heard that one so many times it should be one of the Ten Commandments. But, luck does play a role in everyone's career. That one day when you are in the right place, you create your own luck. **Great Employees** create their own luck—makes a great bumper sticker, "LUCK HAPPENS." You ask any really successful person about his or her career and you'll hear a story about luck. Nobody has made it without luck. Ask Phil Knight, Chairman of Nike, about luck. He will have more than one story to tell (although he probably will not mention that part of that luck came when I was Nike's banker in their early years). Really, I was their banker, but I didn't have the vision. I couldn't figure out why they put that goofy thing on the side of the shoes—also known as a "swoosh."

8. **Politics.** Don't vote! Stay away from the politics at the water cooler. It will be hard, but you must do it. Here are a couple of examples of politics to avoid. First, when the boss has a pet employee, don't get jealous. Remember, there is nothing you can do. Don't try to break it up. Refer to Chapter 6 on bosses.

A second example involves office factions. Let's say that you are working in a department where the manager is going to retire in six months and there are two people in the department jockeying for the position. It is tempting to support one of the two people. Probably you have a closer relationship with one of the individuals and want to throw your support to that person. Fight the temptation. Do not support your friend. Stay neutral.

Avoid acting on and spreading rumors. When it comes to intracompany communication, usually the rumor mill is faster than company announcements, but less accurate. And there are many sources of ammunition for the rumor mill. Think about it for a minute. I'll bet you can come up with five rumors flying around your company at this time. It is always fun to tell an uninformed employee something about the company or its people within the company. Don't do it unless it is "public information." I have seen an employee congratulated for a promotion that had not yet been announced. When it was announced, it wasn't the person who was congratulated prematurely. Think about how badly both people felt.

9. **Promotions.** One of these days, even if you are a **Great Employee,** you are going to get passed up for a promotion. How you handle that "pass" will tell a lot about your future. I have seen both extremes. One is where the employee says "too bad" and goes on about his or her work. The other is where the employee quits working for the company and moves on to something else.

Emotions are really tested when you are passed up for a promotion. Handle it without emotions. Handle it with class. That means you say to yourself, "I would have picked me, but I am not the manager who made the decision." Congratulate the person promoted, with sincerity. Without confronting your boss, ask why you were not selected. In doing so, you can work on improving your skills to be in line for the next promotion. To do both of these, you must work on those emotions. Work to understand that the manager had his or her reasons for choosing someone else. If you find yourself thinking negatively about the decision, turn it off. Then, spend that time working to understand the reasons why the other employee was selected. The way you handle this situation will have a huge impact on your boss, the person promoted, and your fellow employees.

10. ***Change.*** I have observed over the years that employees (and many managers) exhibit a unique type of difficulty with change in the workplace. Change in the workplace can take many different forms: a change in bosses; a transfer to a new department; a physical change in location; the elimination or creation of a department; a new member added to a department. The list goes on and on.

To be a ***Great Employee***, you must master the skill of adapting to change. The first question to ask yourself is, "How will that change impact me?" Then take out a pad and list the changes which will be positive for you in one column. Make another column to list the negatives.

Study the list. The positives should make you very happy and enthusiastic. Now, use that enthusiasm to help you with the negatives. Write out the 3 or 4 things that will help you overcome the negatives. Those now become goals. Once you have your goals you can build a strategy to achieve those goals. By focusing on your goals, you will not get caught up in the difficulties challenging the other employees who don't prepare themselves to handle the change.

"I can do something else besides stuff a ball through a hoop. My biggest resource is my mind."
— Kareem Abdul Jabbar

4

Give Me Some Attitude

You can't make it without it! Don't even try! As I search for the common characteristics of the successful **Great Employee**, I find one trait is absolutely necessary—a positive, friendly, enthusiastic, "get it done" attitude—*an important characteristic!*

To repeat, you simply cannot maximize your potential, your performance, your value as a **Great Employee**, without a bright "can do" attitude. Reread this paragraph if necessary. You cannot maximize your value as a **Great Employee** without a positive attitude.

Ha, ha. It is early in the book, and I've thrown you a curve already. I stated that you cannot be successful without a positive attitude. What did I do? I made my point with a negative statement. Granted, this is a fine point, but it is the fine line that represents the difference between a negative and a positive attitude.

So now let's use a positive statement rather than a negative. You can maximize your value as a **Great Employee** with a positive attitude. All I did was change cannot to can and without to with. What a difference this makes. It's positive and people love positive. Yet, if it is so simple, why do we only observe a few employees who really maintain a positive, charge-ahead attitude? Do you think those employees were born with it? Is it the way they were raised as children? Is it something they see that others do not? Just what is it? Relax and read on. It is all of the above—but most importantly, it is you.

You can make the difference. You can change your attitude from negative to positive or from positive to more positive. It will take about thirty days. By searching for the positive in every situation you can build a habit. A habit is learned and it takes as little as one month. Not a bad investment to change your outlook to positive, positive, positive. Aristotle wrote, *"We are what we repeatedly do. Excellence, then, is not an act, but a habit."* Pretty good philosophy.

The *Great Employees'* Definition of Attitude: Your attitude is in your attitude.

Let's try it. How many times have you heard, "One bad apple can ruin the whole crate?" I have heard that saying so many times I can immediately visualize a round wooden apple crate (like a bushel basket) with old rotten apples dripping juices out of them. I can even smell them.

But how many times have you heard, "One great apple is worth the price of the crate?" Not often, because a majority take the negative approach. Visualize that old wooden crate.

You know what a rotten apple looks like. See them there in the crate. Now, can you imagine reaching into the crate? Gooey, sticky rotten apples. Ah, but in the middle of the crate is a golden apple (not a golden delicious apple, but rather an apple made of gold). The gold would not allow any of the goo to penetrate it. It stood solid—and it was worth the price of the crate.

And what about the old "cup is half full or half empty?" Remember, some people have developed a habit of seeing a cup half full, while others have developed a habit of seeing the cup half empty. It all depends on your attitude.

Look at the illustration on the next page. What do you see? An old woman—or maybe a young woman. It all depends on your perspective. Much like positive versus negative.

By now I hope my point has been made. Attitude is optional. Your attitude is all in your attitude. "Give me a break," you say. "Get on with it. Tell me what it takes. What does it look like? What do you mean 'attitude is all in your attitude?'"

Perhaps a quote from Dale Carnegie might help. Carnegie said, "If half a century of living has taught me anything at all, it has taught me that, "Nothing can bring you peace but yourself.'" See, only you can bring peace to yourself. Likewise, only you can bring a more positive attitude into your life.

The key is to learn to build a positive attitude. It takes training. It takes looking at everything in your life as a positive. My wife likes to call problems "*challenges*." There can be only one reason why she does this—it is all in her

attitude. We need to help you develop that same positive manner to look at things the way the **Great Employee** looks at things. We will, and that's why you paid $10 for this book.

You can develop a habit of maintaining a positive attitude. I once had a salesperson who was good (not great, but good). The only thing holding him back was his negative attitude. This guy could find negative in anything. I was frustrated, because he had lots of potential.

One day, at my wits end, I asked him to go through the newspaper every day for thirty days and bring me five articles a day that covered positive news (and the winning teams from the sports page did not count). His mood changed within a week. By the end of one month, he was a changed man. He developed the habit of being positive. I hasten to add that his sales commissions reflected his positive attitude as well. He is now a **Great Employee**.

I once worked for a company that consisted of many **Great Employees**. Given all of the standard measures of success, there was not one reason why the company should or could be successful. It was undercapitalized. It was in an industry that had too many competitors. It didn't have a unique product, and there wasn't one MBA on staff.

What did the company have? It had a cadre of people who exercised positive thinking. When things looked really bleak somebody would say, "Okay, time for **terrific**." At that point we would all shout, "**Terrific**," three times. So now you as a reader, it is time for **terrific**. Try it. Try saying, "**Terrific**," three times out loud.

Okay, great. Now let's try saying it with some feeling, some meaning, get some heart into it. Think of a bluer sky, a brighter sun. Envision something that translates to **terrific**. Maybe it's the thrill of victory, the feeling of accomplishment. Now say, "**Terrific!**" Come on, don't be shy. Add some volume. Now one more time, add more volume and see that sky, smell that salty air of the beach. Okay, the third and last time, "**Terrific! Terrific! Terrific!**" At this point I know you feel better. If you don't, send me your book, you get your money back. A fellow named Benjamin Disraeli said, "Every production of genius must be the production of enthusiasm."

"**Terrific! Terrific! Terrific!**" is a simple exercise that will help you develop, or remind yourself, of a way to make yourself feel better. Hey, wait a minute. What's this about feeling better? You mean, if I feel better I will have that attitude that will help me be a better employee? You bet. You got it. That's it, folks. Simple as that: self-harmony, self-esteem and self-confidence. Feeling better about yourself will help you become a ***Great Employee***.

None of us is really that much different from the other. Do you think the person at work with the sincere smile, the cheery disposition and the positive outlook gets up in the morning that way? Ready to charge ahead and leap tall buildings with a single bound? No way! These exceptions (the ***Great Employee*** is an exception), are just like you and me. They don't like the sound of the alarm on Monday (or Tuesday, for that matter). They are not ready to step in the bus, train, or car at the required time. They may not even be ready to go to work at the necessary time.

But they do one thing that separates them from the average employee. They wake up and warm up. They know it is going to take a while to get into the groove. Do you think the *Great Employee* wakes up with a smile, jumps out of bed, exercises, drinks a glass of orange juice and downs granola? No way, man. It takes roughly 90 minutes to wake up and become alert. That's why fashion models don't have photo shoots in the early morning. Nothing before 9 a.m. Waking up is the reverse of becoming tired and falling asleep. You don't immediately become tired at day's end. Depending on your schedule, you probably start to become tired about 8 p.m. And during the next couple of hours you become more tired and finally fall asleep. Well, waking up is the same process. So remember, you have roughly 90 minutes to prepare yourself for the day.

You now know that *Great Employees* don't wake up that way. But during those critical 90 minutes, they prepare themselves for the day ahead. They start thinking positively. They start planning the two or three things they can do to make the day a good one. They start to think about the things that could make for a bad day. Things like, "What about my boss who is really negative ? What about the ridiculous report that must be finished today? What about Mark or Jennifer, who, again today, will not cooperate with the rest of the staff?"

Who cares? Boss negative? I will be positive and it will rub off. Believe you me, I'm gonna make that sucker smile today. And maybe twice tomorrow. Report due today? Get tough, come on. Any third grader alive has had to put up with some "stupid report." Now to Mark and Jennifer who don't cooperate, who gossip, who won't carry their share. It is always going to be that way. Every office, every warehouse, every retail floor has a Mark and a Jennifer. They aren't going to change, or are they? You may have the power. You and your positive attitude can change anything and anybody. You will win out in time. Negative attitudes lose. Positive attitudes win.

Man, you want to talk about positive attitude: A good friend of mine is always up, always happy, always smiling, always friendly and most importantly, always performing at a level far beyond his fellow employees.

Finally, I asked him, "Why is it you are always so positive? You're separated from your wife. The company you work for is not doing that great. You were just in a major car accident. How do you do it?" I expected some profound response. One I could use to make me a positive person with an attitude that truly glows. His answer blew me away. He said, "I don't allow my brain to accept anything that is negative." I was a banker at the time and, if you know bankers, you know that I could not comprehend what he was saying. It took me a couple of years and several books on positive thinking until I learned how he did it. He developed a habit of not listening to negative talk or thinking negative thoughts. That is exactly what made him a **Great Employee**.

I mentioned earlier in this chapter that I was with a company that had no reason to succeed. But we did and we did it with attitude. We found that attitude could solve almost any problem.

Every member of that team believed that working with a positive attitude could accomplish anything. It would take hard work, cooperation, give and take, set backs, tons of brain energy, execution and defeat at times. But together we maintained an attitude that could be felt when you walked into the conference room. That company has grown from annual sales of forty million dollars to over three hundred million dollars in six years.

The only reason it succeeded was because it had *Great Employees* everywhere you looked. From the warehouse, to the sales floor, to advertising, to accounting, to the boardroom, it had employees with great, positive, enthusiastic attitudes. And you know what? These people are the same as you and me. These people learned to become *Great Employees.*

From this chapter, we want you to learn how to maintain an improved positive attitude. Here are your *Great Employees' 10 Tips On:*

Improving Your Attitude

1.   **Start your day by devoting the first 10 minutes to yourself. Remember, you are a great and wonderful person.**

2.   **Focus on your strengths. There is not another person in the world like you.**

3.   **Look in a mirror. See yourself as a better person today than yesterday.**

4. *Think positive thoughts about yourself. This is your time to get your engine started.*

5. *Now, spend about 10 minutes thinking about what lies ahead for you today. Try to identify any challenges you may encounter today. Now you will be better prepared.*

6. *Say to yourself, "Today is the most important day in my life."*

7. *Look for the positive in everything around you. If you read about a plane crash where 50 people die and 10 live, focus on the fact that 10 survived.*

8. *Remember, positive thinking is a habit. You are going to further develop that habit today.*

9. *Focus on the people you will work with today. Find the positive in those people. Try to find more positive in them every day.*

10. *Say to yourself, "Now I am prepared for the day. I have prepared my attitude to maximize my performance as a Great Employee."*

"One kind word can warm three winter months."
— Japanese Proverb

5
Can We Talk?

*E*ver think how we would get along in life without the ability to communicate? Obviously not very well. But, given the importance of communicating, it's amazing that we don't work harder at it.

I've often thought, "Why don't the schools teach children how to communicate before they try teaching them to read?" Maybe "reading, writing and arithmetic" should be "listening, talking and understanding?"

I know that communication is part of the subject called English, as well as the subject of speech. However, diagramming sentences didn't help me much with communicating. And my first speech class wasn't until college. By that time. it was almost too late. If you've heard one of my presentations, you might say it was too late.

I had to give my first speech in 1966. I was so uninformed I thought Toastmasters was a high quality toaster. So, I wrote a speech (outlined as the textbook required). This was going to be a speech like no one had ever heard (and it was). I went to the front of the class to get ready to talk, or, as the professor said, "speak." By the time I got there, my jaw had locked. No way would it move. My knees were shaking so badly that if I could have talked, it would have sounded like I was driving over eighty miles of rough road. It was brutal.

(A quick note: Did you know that speaking in front of a group ranks number one on our list of things that frighten us?)

Let's get back to communicating. It's very different from giving a public speech. Let's talk about the key elements of communicating that make it seem so difficult. But let me assure you, that when you have finished this chapter you will have the tools to communicate like a *Great Employee.*

The *Great Employees'* Definition of Communication: Stop, look and listen—then talk.

Stop for a moment and think about a situation at work where you are talking with your boss. The topic of conversation is *his* boss. Now, you know that your boss dislikes his boss. But you really like your boss's boss. You are at lunch, and the purpose of the lunch is so your boss can vent his frustrations about his boss. Confused, read once more.

Okay, ready for some stress! You must be true to yourself. But on the other hand, you don't want to argue with your boss about his boss. Yet your boss wants feedback. Let's make it even more stressful, your boss is about to get promoted to another department, and with the promotion you will get his job.

What are you faced with? I'll tell you. First, you had better select your words perfectly. And you had better arrange those word in sentences and paragraphs so they say exactly what you mean. Next, you had better make sure that your tone and voice inflection communicate your meaning.

That's just the vocal part of your responses. Now let's add some body language. Raising of the eyebrows, hand gestures, looking up, down or away. And then there is "attitude," that subverbal stuff that is so hard to explain. Don't you wish you were somewhere else? Here is how your comment may sound four different ways:

I'm not suggesting he is a great boss.
I'm not *suggesting* he is a great boss.
I'm not suggesting he is a *great* boss.
I'm not suggesting he is a great *boss*.

From the examples above, I think you will agree that the verbal side of communicating is not an easy task. Fact is, it is darn tough to make sure we mean what we say. But to become a **Great Employee,** we must mean what we say.

Now let's talk about the other side of communicating—*listening*. I had a friend tell me, "You have two ears and one mouth—use them in that proportion." Just like in speaking, listening has its challenges.

How well do you listen? Before you respond, think about the last time you were introduced to a stranger. Bet you the price of the book, you didn't remember his or her first and last name. Well, maybe not the price of the book, but a least a dime.

When you meet someone for the first time, there are lots of distractions. One is visual—you know, those things that close off your ability to listen. You are thinking about the funny plaid tie the gentleman is wearing or the funny plaid tie you are wearing. Another distraction is the fact that you want to make sure you say your name so they will hear it. So you go a couple of octaves lower so it sounds like you're saying your name in the shower.

Man, this communication stuff is getting complicated. Let me see if I have this straight:

First, I have to say exactly what I mean. Then the listener has to make sure he or she understands exactly what I said. Then, he or she has to communicate exactly what they mean.

And then, I have to make sure I understand exactly what they said.

Maybe those teachers do have the right idea. *"Let's teach reading, writing, and arithmetic—it's a heck of a lot easier than communication."*

Let me tell you a communication story that really taught me about listening and understanding. When I was a ripe old age of 22, I was "helping" in the garage with my then father-in-law. This guy was a mechanics' mechanic. He was teaching me all about a truck's points, plugs, and condenser. At 22, I had graduated from college, and I worked for a bank, which meant I read the *Wall Street Journal*. Now, with "all that education," I was trying to be cool and still learn about plugs, points and condensers.

It was winter. Father-in-law "Chuck" had mounted a heating fan from the ceiling in the corner of his garage. Between that and some Irish Whiskey, we were quite toasty— I thought.

Chuck's 6'4" body is almost entirely under the hood of a '62 Ford pickup, changing the points. He yells at this college graduate to "turn the fan." I figure he must be cold, but I didn't know why. He yells out once more, "Turn the fan." So I climb up on the workbench and try to turn this fan so it will blow the hot air on him. But he is under the hood of the pickup with only his rear end exposed.

Remember, I am listening to this guy carefully, because I want him to know I am smart—because I am a banker and I read the *Wall Street Journal.* Now in contrast, Chuck had no college degree and is a millwright. (When you are 22, a college degree is quite important.)

So here is my father-in-law, who is, under the hood of a pickup with his rear end sticking out, telling me to "turn the fan." By this time it is, "Turn the @!%#! fan." And here am I up on the workbench trying to turn this @!%#! fan which is bolted to the ceiling to withstand the worst San Francisco earthquakes. The garage could have come down, but this fan would remain.

About that time, ol' Chuck backs out from under the hood of the pickup and says, "What the @!%#! are you doing up there on my workbench?" I respond by saying, "I'm trying to turn this @!%#! fan of yours." Then he says, "Not that fan, you @!%#! idiot, the fan in the truck. I am trying to set the points."

That incident taught me more about the complexities of communication than four years of college.

There is nothing the **Great Employee** can do to change the necessities and the challenges associated with communicating. The only thing we can do is to try to simplify it.

Therefore, we are going to review the different levels of communication we are faced with during an average day at work. It seems like we talk to a lot of people during the day. And we do. However, we communicate with five categories of people:

1. Ourselves.
2. Employees at levels of responsibility below ours.
3. Employees at our level of responsibility.
4. Employees at levels of responsibility above ours.
5. Outsiders.

To keep it halfway simple, let's remember we must listen and talk. So let's put it all together to give you the **Great Employees' 10 Tips On:**

Communicating

1. **When talking to yourself, let it all hang out.** You can say anything you want to yourself. You can say things to yourself you would never say in public. (Just make sure your lips don't move.)

2. **Listen to yourself.** Now this is important. When you find yourself listening to yourself, be careful. Do not listen to those negative things you are talking about. Just say to yourself, "I have already said that once, so now it is time to talk about something else—something positive."

3. **When talking to employees who are in levels of responsibility below yours, do not talk down to them.** It is so easy to do. Remember these people are the ones who support you. Be careful not to walk over them.

4. *When listening to employees in a level of responsibility below yours—be all ears.* They frequently know what is going on out there before you do. A good friend of mine has managed several large companies successfully. His secret to success has been his ability to listen to the folks on the firing line.

5. *When talking to peers, do not try to impress them to prove that they are really not your peers.* Talk is cheap. What you do on the job will impress your peers ten billion times more than what you say.

6. *When listening to peers, refer to Tip #5 and reverse it.* Have patience. Hear them out. If they think or say something important that you didn't, compliment them.

7. ***When talking to an employee with a level of responsibility above yours, be yourself.*** Remember, you start with 10 points. If you say the wrong thing, you are down to 9 points. But don't worry—the closer you are to being a *Great Employee*, the easier you will find these exchanges.

8. ***When listening to an employee with a level of responsibility above yours, do not let an earthquake interfere with what he or she is saying.*** Focus on their comments. Try to understand why they are making them. And, do not, under any circumstances, let them intimidate you. If they try, brush it aside. Ignore it.

9. ***When talking to someone outside the company, choose your words wisely.*** You represent the company at all times. Being critical of the company to outsiders is not something that people want to hear. It is considered "complaining." Focus on the positive.

10. ***When listening to someone outside the company, maintain an open mind.*** Just keep your ears peeled.

"Thou shalt labor for thy boss."

— Shakespeare

6

Be a Boss Booster!

H ow many books have you read on management? During my thirty plus years as an employee, I would guess I have read more than twenty. Most of them have been written by someone who had been part of a management consulting group or someone with a Ph.D. in business or psychology. A few were written by someone who was an outstanding president or CEO of a major company.

For the most part, I've learned from each book. But to tell you the truth, too many involved theory, new management approaches, or too many charts and graphs. I personally think that the reason the *One Minute Manager* was so successful was because it was written in a simple fashion, easily understood and applied.

I had wanted to write this book for several years. It was only recently that all that dreaming became reality. During this span of several years, I have asked countless friends and business associates the same question, "How many books have you read on management?" The responses would vary, but most would guess ten to twenty.

Then I would ask them, "How many books have you read on being a *Great Employee*?" All had the same response, "None." Presently, when I am asked about the nature of my book, I respond with the same questions-and-answer routine. At the end of the exchange, I always receive the same response, "That's a great idea."

The purpose of this book is 100% employee-driven. As you read through it, I think you will agree it is not written to help managers become better managers, but to help employees become better employees, or as I like to call them, *Great Employees.*

There may be some confusion here. Some people are employees without anyone reporting to them. Others are bosses who report to a boss. In both cases, they are employees. For those bosses who read this book, and especially this chapter, I hope the information will help you become a better employee for your boss.

With the information you receive in this chapter, you will be able to help your boss become a better boss. By using the *Great Employees' 10 Tips on Boosting Your Boss,* you will be amazed on how much you can improve your boss's performance. With that in mind, let's look at a different definition of a boss.

**The *Great Employees'* Definition of a Boss:
That Person To Whom I Report, Who Needs All
the Help I Can Possibly Provide.**

And, this is extremely important, if not obvious, *"If you help your boss succeed, you will succeed."* This is not a selfish "brown nosing" kind of statement. The fact is that the position of manager is a darn tough job. Let's examine some of the reasons why.

First, think about how bosses are chosen. Typically, they are chosen from a group of candidates who have performed well in their current positions. Those candidates were, in all likelihood, very good at doing their current jobs, which may not have been managerial positions. In other words, they are probably very good at whatever the company does. In retailing, it is usually a salesperson. In banking it is usually a loan officer. In manufacturing, it is usually someone from the production line.

To perform well in their current jobs, the employees probably received a substantial amount of training. When I was a banker, I trained in a variety of departments to prepare me to become a commercial loan officer. It was two years before I made my first loan. At that time, we also went through a week-long training session on selling bank services. But, after a couple more years, I was promoted to a management position, with eighty or so people working for me. How much training did I have to prepare me for that position? *None!*

It isn't that senior management of most companies doesn't realize the importance of well-trained managers. Many companies make it a high priority. But, more often than not, there just seem to be too many other requirements for managers' time. "We have schedules to keep." "We must push advertising." "We have got to get that project completed by

Monday." "We are really pressed for time, there is no way to fit it in."

How does this impact you? As mentioned earlier, it means your boss needs your help. Whatever your job description is, it should never change. It should always be *to help your boss.*

But to be able to do that, you must develop an understanding of your boss's capabilities. Realize that he or she may not be a great boss because he or she had not been sufficiently trained. One doesn't become a great boss simply by being promoted into the position. It takes a lot of training and experience which usually take years to accomplish. As an employee, try to accept the above and become more understanding of your boss's abilities and inabilities. Once you do that, it will open a gigantic door for both of you—a door which will enable you to provide your boss with much more help in "getting the job done."

Benjamin Franklin said it well when he said, *"Any fool can criticize, condemn and complain—and most fools do."* So don't be a fool. I have been there. It pays no dividends. It gets you nowhere. Instead, the *Great Employees'* three "Cs" are Cooperation, Consideration, and Compassion.

Understanding that bosses are not born but rather, created, and accepting that it is your job is to help your boss are the two cornerstones for building the *Great Employees'* **10 Tips for:**

Boosting the Boss

1. *Many bosses need further training in management.* Larry Wilson, Chairman of the Pecos River Learning Centers has a great approach. He says when your boss errs, don't call him or her an S.O.B., but rather an F.H.B. That stands for a *fallible human being.* It means that everybody makes mistakes. Accept mistakes or errors and go on about the task at hand which is helping your boss.

2. *Criticizing your boss is not helping your boss.* It is said that if your boss criticizes you once, it takes ten acts of praise to erase the hurt felt by the criticism. I think that goes both ways. When a boss makes a mistake, it takes ten acts of perfection before the mistake is forgotten.

We talked about this earlier. I once worked for a company where we did not criticize mistakes. To make a mistake was no big deal. When it happened, we studied it to improve our performance. We blamed no one. This approach fostered creativity, change and improvement. It was one of the main reasons the company was so successful.

3. *Time spent understanding your boss and his or her decisions is time well spent.* Often employees don't have the same amount of information the boss has. Without that information, a boss's decision or action may seem "ridiculous."

Here is an example of me being critical of the advertising department of a company I was with. We had an annual sale where we mailed out about 250,000 mailers promoting the event. It was called a "blanket mailing." We had done this for several years. Word spread through the company that this year we were only going to send out about 125,000 mailers. I, along with most of the sales staff, thought the sale would be a disaster. When the day of the sale arrived, we happily found we were wrong. We had a record day. What we did not know was that the advertising department had purchased a computer program which sent mailers to only those customers who were more likely to purchase our product. By not sending out a "blanket mailing," the company saved money and increased sales.

4. *Great Employees anticipate their bosses needs.* This is when work can really get fun. Remember the television show M.A.S.H.

Colonel Potter would yell out for his assistant "Radar!" and Radar would already be there. Radar had a sixth sense, and he always knew what the colonel wanted, which was obviously how he got the nickname. But that's TV. In the real world, anticipating your boss's expectations requires you to really study your boss. How does he plan for things? When does she do her best work? What is he a stickler for? What kinds of patterns can you recognize in your boss?

Once you know your boss's requirements, you can go the extra mile, before he or she asks. It also demonstrates that you are thinking ahead. The ability to think ahead or work ahead is one of the most important characteristics of the *Great Employee.* When you read the Chapter 8, which contains quotes, look for it. Both employees and bosses say a *Great Employee* is one who does more than is asked or expected.

5. *Great Employees learn from their bosses.* Have you ever made this statement? "I learned more of what not to do than what to do from that boss." The key to benefiting from this is to learn without being critical or emotional. Don't get frustrated, agitated, or all boiled up.

I had a boss who had absolutely no communication skills. He had a tough time talking before a group of people. In one-on-one conversations he was no better. He wouldn't look you in the eye. He wouldn't give clear instructions. He never took the time to explain why this or that was important. He drove me nuts. However, by having that boss, I realized how important communciation skills were. Had that boss maintained average communication skills, I would not have focused as hard on the importance of communication in the work place. My only error was to let his inabilities frustrate me. Believe me, stay cool. It really pays off.

6. **Bosses actions are not always what you may think they are.** Too many of us dwell on the negative, especially when it comes to our bosses' reactions or comments. Earlier, I told you that for every negative comment from your boss it takes ten positives to "make it right." That is because we take a boss's comments so seriously. Combine that with our desire to please and we can get pretty worked up at times when the boss says something critical.

Learn how to handle criticism from your boss. I've worked with bosses who threw things and with bosses who never showed anger. Frequently, the guy who threw things did not get as mad as the guy who showed no anger. But in each case, I took their criticism much harder than it was delivered. Typically, when you think your boss is upset with you, he or she is not as upset as you think. Remember that—it may help you from dwelling on the negative.

7. *Make your boss look good.* Over the last thirty years, I have seen that the one pattern that always prevails is, *"If you help your boss succeed, you will succeed."* As employees move up the flag pole they always remember who helped them get there. And usually they will call upon those same people to help them again. You see this in sports. What was the first thing the University of Oregon's head football coach did when he was hired as head coach for the Rams? He hired two assistant coaches from the university to go with him. Those two assistants obviously made Coach Brooks look great.

8. ***Remember, your boss usually has a boss.*** Keep in mind that your boss probably has to go through the same kinds of things you go through with him or her. The formal channels of communication in a company are slower than the grapevine. This is important for you to know. The employees always spot a boss not doing his or her job before management does. When I was an employee, I noticed it took management about six months to catch up. Be patient!

9. ***Great Employees never get mad at their bosses.*** They know better. There will come a time when you feel you deserve to be mad. Get that out of your mind. Having a "mad on" at the boss will show up in an instant. It will ruin your performance faster than you could ever deliberately "mess up."

10. ***Great Employees make great bosses great.*** A boss can't possibly be great unless he or she has a team of ***Great Employees***. That takes us back to our definition of the Boss, "That person to whom I report, who needs all the help I can possibly provide."

"Your customer signs your paycheck."
Frank Cooper

"Your customer is everyone you work with."
Walt Mulvey

7

Who Is the Customer?

How many times are you a customer in one day? Ever stop to think about it? Well, to put the importance of being a customer in the proper perspective, let's try to count.

Start when you wake up in the morning to the alarm clock. You bought the alarm clock or clock radio, so that makes you a customer. We can even count the sheets, covers, and bedspread that are on your mattress, that is on your bed frame that you bought. And the bed is on the floor of your home or apartment which you pay for monthly. Now you are halfway awake so you put on your robe and slippers and walk into the bathroom and turn on the lights, thanks to the electric company. Keep in mind that you bought the robe, slippers, and lightbulbs. Now you turn on the shower—thanks to the gas company. Here comes the water, thanks to the city or municipality. Now to the soap, the washrag, the shampoo, and the conditioner. Then to the razor (face or legs). Guys— try shaving in the shower, it's great. Next is the towel. Now the glasses or contacts. Then to the TV to hit the early morning news, which comes on the cable. Then the toothbrush and toothpaste. Now to the hair dryer, comb or brush (probably both). Time for mousse and hair spray. Makeup for the ladies. Aftershave for the guys and perfume for the gals. Okay, we haven't even gotten out of the bathroom and we have been a customer 33 times. By the time you get to work, it will be well over 100 times.

Now what happens when a few of the above "necessities of life" don't work quite right? We are all faced with the frustrations of not being treated well as a customer. It happens to us on a daily basis. It is simply a function of our society. We rely on so many different products and services to assist us in our daily living because we have become an interdependent society. That means the odds of a failure in a product or service are huge. I'm sure that you are faced with a customer service problem of some sort every day.

This creates inconvenience for us and, typically, frustration. After all, we are exposed to thousands of advertisements during a typical day. All of these advertisements suggest the same thing: "Buy our product or service." They also suggest that the product is of high quality. You have never been exposed to an advertisement that suggests the product is, "Okay, but you might have some problems with it." Of course not. But there are thousands of products out there that are "just okay," and you may very well have problems with them. I certainly hope your company or organization is not one of those with customer service problems because of a lack of quality in your product or service.

Because of advertising, we have been conditioned to expect the best. When I was in the furniture business, I learned that the customer who purchased a $399 sofa expected the same level of quality as did the customer who purchased the $2000 sofa. Therefore, we had to provide the same quality of customer service to both customers.

When we are faced with a problem in a product or service, we become frustrated, and maybe angry. Then we take out our anger on the employee representing the company that produced the product or service. I have had to interact with my share of unhappy customers over my 30 years in business. And they all want the same thing—a solution to the problem the product or service is creating.

Customer service can be *proactive* or *reactive*. *Proactive* is when you or your company provide a consistently superior product or service which does not require any followup. The proactive companies are full of **Great Employees**. *Reactive* companies are those that are constantly "putting out fires." Their product or service is of a quality that requires them to go back and make corrections to it.

I come from the Pacific Northwest, the home of Nordstrom's. Here is a company that has never once advertised their superior customer service program. And it seems that their service is the one which hundreds of companies want to emulate.

There is another company in the Northwest which is gaining an outstanding customer service reputation that rivals Nordstrom's. The name of the company is Les Schwab Tires. A tire store? Yup! The people in their stores actually run rather than walk. If you buy tires from Les Schwab, you think you are the only customer in the store. And you can see and feel the camaraderie between their employees. *Both of these companies are much smarter than their competitors because they put their money into the development of* **Great Employees**. Their dollars are better spent on people rather than on advertising.

Your company must be committed to customer service. If it is not, it will show up like Cindy Crawford's mole. You will see it externally and internally. I wish the term "word of mouth" could be better understood by advertising agencies. More companies need to take money out of the advertising budgets and put it into the customer service budget and employee training. We would have fewer ads to suffer through and better customer service to enjoy.

Okay, so we know how customer service problems are created. And we know that the odds are quite high that we will experience one daily. Now let's define your customer. I'll give you a hint, it is not just the person or who purchases or uses your company's or organization's product.

The *Great Employees'* Definition of a Customer: Anyone in Your Company Who Depends on Your Performance.

There is so much written about customer service as it relates to the traditional customer. So let's just focus on the customers you interface with at work—your fellow employees, those people you work with every day or perhaps only once or twice a month. Let's look at all of the people at work as customers needing something from you. Talk about supply and demand. Think of yourself as being the supply and the entire company being the demand. Makes you feel pretty important, doesn't it? It should!

Now take a minute to think about that last statement. It will help you immensely from this day on. If you provide "Nordstrom's" service to your customers, you could be as successful as Nordstrom's.

Let's reflect on our experiences as customers, demanding product perfection and superior customer service. And let's adapt some of those "customer service rules" for the workplace. Here are the *Great Employees' 10 Tips for:*

Customer Service In the Workplace

1. *Set the Stage.* When someone helps you at your favorite store, it is nice to know that they sincerely want to be of service. Therefore, you want to make sure *your* customer (fellow employee) knows you are anxious to help. And you should be. Here is an opportunity to contribute and learn; a chance to interact with other people in your company. Here is a chance to demonstrate your initiative and enthusiasm. Once your fellow employees knows you want to help "get it done," they become more relaxed. This is important, because a relaxed meeting promotes better communication. *Great Employees* set the stage so maximum communication can produce maximum results.

2.   *Know Their Names.* Don't you love it when an employee at the cleaners or grocery store calls you by name. The importance of knowing people's names cannot be over-emphasized. It tells them that you care enough to know their names. *Great Employees* work on knowing the names of as many co-workers as possible. It suggests you value them as more than just cogs in the machinery. You may use first name or last name depending upon your relationship with the person. In recent years, the use of first names has become much more accepted, regardless of title. Most managers I know would rather be called by their first names. So, regardless of their positions in the company, call them by name.

3.   *Listen, Listen, Listen.* Listening and hearing are not the same. How about the waiter who hears that you want steak well done and he brings it to you rare. He lapsed for just one second and didn't listen. Effective listening is difficult under the best of circumstances. You may want to refer to Chapter 5 on communication to brush up on listening. Much of your communication between departments is done over the phone where you can be easily distracted. Make sure you are asking yourself, "Am I getting the *real* message?" Tell yourself to listen. Remember there is no relationship between intelligence and listening skills. I have seen more people become **Great Employees** based upon their listening skills than based upon their intelligence.

Often you are talking or working with an employee who is considered a boss. That can create some anxiety which has a negative effect on your ability to concentrate and listen. Stay relaxed! These folks are just like you and me. The better you listen, the more relaxed you will become.

4. ***Respect Other Employees' Requests.*** Why? Earlier in this chapter, we talked about how customers expect the product or service *your company* provides to work with all the quality they expect. Remember, we have been programmed to expect product perfection. So at work we expect the same. When we ask another employee to do something that will help in the process, we expect his or her performance to have the same high quality that we would produce. Your performance is not going to be of the highest quality if you do not respect your fellow employee's requests. Perhaps you don't respect a request because you don't completely understand it. If that is the case, go back and ask for more time to listen and for the opportunity to ask questions.

5. ***Ask Lots of Questions.*** When you make a big important purchase, you usually need some help with it. Let's say you are going to buy a new television. There are over 40 questions a salesperson should ask you before he or she has enough information to recommend the best TV to meet your needs and budget. It's the same way at work—the more you know about the situation or the task, the more you may be able to contribute. Remember, often the workplace is quite busy and employees may feel stressed so they don't give you all the information you need to do the job of a ***Great Employee.***

6. ***Be positive.*** Think about the satisfaction that you feel when your boss compliments you on your work. "That is a great job, thank you for doing it." Those words can make you feel so good, so positive. Try to maintain that feeling as much as possible. We talked about the importance of a positive attitude in Chapter 4. ***Great Employees*** do everything they can to stay positive. They know that they can do a better job with a positive attitude. To make sure they maintain that "get it done attitude" they use the 10 Tips found in Chapter 4. Remember you must find positive in everything you do. So stay positive, and your customers will love you for it.

7. *Forget the Blame.* Too often when something at work doesn't work, we get caught up in blaming somebody for it. Strip that word from your vocabulary. Blaming people doesn't help. It is negative energy. Stay focused on the customer. *Great Employees* know the most important thing they can do is to get the job done. That is what is going to serve the customer the most. A small suggestion to someone later on may be all it takes to prevent a problem from happening again.

8. *Go Beyond the Customer's Expectations.* Refer back to Tip #6. This is your chance to really shine. Customers have grown accustomed to expecting outstanding products or service. When they get it, they like it. It feels good. In Chapter 8, you will read quotes from both managers and employees on what it takes to be a *Great Employee*. A common thread running through their quotes is, "Do more than is expected." Do it, and customers will beat a path to your door.

9. ***If Necessary, Don't Hesitate to Apologize.*** Sometimes, regardless of how hard you try, you just can't do the job that is expected. Like that waiter with the rare steak. He may have taken a hundred orders that night. This could have been his only mistake. We all make mistakes, and we all make plenty of them. Sometimes it is the hardest worker who is making the most mistakes. As long as he or she learns from the mistakes, it is okay. Just make sure you apologize and try to discover what would get the job done as expected, next time. And focus on what you learned from the experience.

10. ***Always Say Thanks.*** "Thanks for doing a great job." I love that sound! Thanks is the most powerful word in our vocabulary. At work, it is not just the manager who should say thanks once in awhile. You need to do it too. How often do you go to your boss and say, "Thanks for helping me out today. I really appreciated that." Certainly you have experienced a great week at work for various reasons. That's the time to go to the boss and say something like, "Great week, we really had it going. Thanks." Your boss is your customer, too.

"I am looking for a lot of men who have an infinite capacity to not know what can't be done."

— Henry Ford

8

Bosses and Great Employees

*T*his chapter contains quotes from old friends and old friends' friends. Some are bosses, some are *Great Employees*. Some are famous, some are not. But in each and every case, there is a pearl of wisdom condensed into a couple of sentences. Go for it, grab the pearls!

*"A **Great Employee** feels a part of the business, feels committed emotionally and professionally to the success of the enterprise. Nurturing this feeling of belonging and caring about that success is key to developing **Great Employees**."*

— Philip M. Hawley, Retired Chairman, CEO, Carter, Hawley, Hale Stores; Director of AT&T, Atlantic Richfield, Bank of America, Johnson & Johnson, and Weyerhaeuser Company

*"**Great Employees** strive for excellence from themselves and their supervisors, anticipate future requirements of their positions, act as a sounding board for new ideas, and are willing to challenge the status quo."*

— DaveWebber, Strategic Planner

*"My definition of a **Great Employee** is one who brings a true "**willing spirit**" to the workplace. Yes, with loyalty, dependability, and a positive attitude, but especially with a **willingness** to do what is asked in the very best way they know how."*

— Phil Jensen, President, Luhr Jensen Fishing Luhrs

*"A **Great Employee** is a person who is inspirational to those he or she works with and follows his or her own aspirations. They can always see the rainbow at the end of the darkest day. They create a sense of security for those not so secure. They have a sense of drive and face all obstacles that might be placed before them. You will always shine if you do the best you can."*

— Heidi R. Beck, Marketing Consultant

*"**Great Employees** know there is no finish line."*

— Phil Knight, Chairman and CEO, Nike

*"The **Great Employee** is one who can understand the needs and emotions of the client."*

— Lawrence Black, President, Black & Company; Member, New York Stock Exchange

*"**Great Employees** know the importance of attendance and hard work. They offer their services to help the employer grow without asking, "What do I get for it?"*

— Gertrude Boyle, Chairwoman, Columbia Sportswear

*"To me, **Great Employees** are the ones who take pride in what they do because they always strive to do their best. **Great Employees** are willing to perform beyond what is expected of them, to take the initiative and do what needs to be done."*

— Cindy Frances, Administrative Assistant

*"There is an old saying in the agriculture industry—the day ends when the job is done. **Great Employees** will focus on what needs to be accomplished and not so much on how much time they put in."*

— Robert Jaedicke, Professor (Emeritus) and Former Dean of Stanford University Graduate School of Business

"To me it is quite basic. **Great Employees** *always do more than they are asked."*

— Neil Goldschmidt, Former Mayor of Portland, Oregon; Former Governor of Oregon; Former U.S. Secretary of Transportation; now Businessman

"A **Great Employee** *is a 'partner,' and partners win together, lose together, share successes and failures. They don't worry about who gets the credit or the blame—as long as the enterprise moves forward. Partnership, like marriage is a two-way street."*

— John von Schlegell, Managing Partner, Endeavour Capital

*"***Great Employees** *are those who, in doing their job well, improve not only their own lives and situations, but benefit their supervisors, departments, and companies as a whole."*

Susan Troldall, Advertising Producer

*"***Great Employee** *are like blockers or tacklers on a football team. They do their best every day. They are there to support the team."*

— Pat Terrell, Founder, Leading Technologies Computer Company

"It may seem strange, but in these days of RIFs, forced early retirements, layoffs, and increasing part-time employment, I still value loyalty above all other employee attributes—loyalty to the company and to me. Perhaps, on the other hand, that's to be expected since it's an increasingly rare commodity."

— Robert Ames, Vice Chairman,
First Interstate Bank of Oregon, N.A.

*"**Great Employees** are those who go beyond what is asked of them—those who go one step further."*

— Jennifer Allers, Media Buyer

*"**Great Employees** care as much about their customers, fellow employees and the company as they do themselves. **Great Employees** like making the customer happy."*

— Phil Wick, President and CEO, Les Schwab Tire Company

*"**Great Employees** exhibit these four leadership traits: initiative, dependability, enthusiasm, and loyalty."*

— Patrick Stickle, President, *The Oregonian*

*"**Great Employees** clearly understand what's most important and the latitude they have to make things happen. They continually demonstrate flexibility and the ability to get it done with a great attitude."*

— Roger Dow, Executive Vice President, Marriott Hotels, Author and Speaker

*"More than anything else, attitude is the attribute that leads to greatness. If an employee's attitude is one of 'can do' rather than 'can't do' or 'it's not part of my job,' he or she will succeed and may become a **Great Employee**."*

— Dennis Pixton, Managing Partner, Moss Adams, Certified Public Accountants

*"**Great Employees** are passionate about their work and reflect their enthusiasm internally and externally. They exhibit a 'can do,' solutions-oriented, positive attitude which is a great way for employees to impact their workplace."*

— Mark Loder, Television Sales Rep

*"A **Great Employee** is a winner with a positive attitude, committed to the team effort, but focused on his or her area of responsibility"*

— Dave Milner, General Manager KEX Radio

*"A **Great Employee** is someone who goes the extra mile—one who takes "ownership" and responsibility for the company without being directly compensated as an "owner" or CEO. He or she becomes a teammate and strives to accomplish all the goals and tasks that are set by the team."*

— Neil Lomax, N.F.L. San Diego Charger Quarterback; now President of Promax, a company committed to helping young people

*"A **Great Employee** is one who can challenge his or her supervisors, yet understand the importance of discretion and showing outward support, despite the boss's shortcomings."*

— Lee Koehn, President, Koehn and Associates Executive Search

*"**Great Employees** are ones who forget about the clock and can focus on the tasks to be done without socializing. They must be willing to manage a million dollar business as if it was their own, regardless of job description."*

— Martin Eberle, President, M.J. Eberle Co.

*"People who will do anything to achieve their goal to be number one. The **Great Employee** is a self starter, intense, confident, focused, enthusiastic and is a great role model. To me, the **Great Employee** radiates success."*

— Skip Williams, Employee turned Entrepreneur

"Make sure your managers establish the parameters under which you can operate. Then become an entrepreneur within those parameters."

— Glen Grodem, Chairman, Smith's Home Furnishings

*"I believe a **Great Employee** is one who can listen well, extract what his manager is asking for, and then perform his or her task beyond the manager's expectations."*

— Jason Palumbis, Ex-Stanford quarterback, Ex-Professional Football Player; Currently, Merchandising Manager

*"**Great Employees** are those who take extreme pride in their work. **Great Employees** are prompt, always giving one hundred percent of their time. They are willing to work late, never complain, help their fellow employees, and always consider the company first, even before themselves."*

— Jim Werre, Sales Trainer

*"**Great Employees** make Great Bosses. You can't be a great leader without great followers."*

— Vince Lombardi, Jr., Speaker and Author

*"**Great Employees** recognize the importance of understanding who both their internal and external customers are and how best to meet their needs. **Great Employees** listen and try to be proactive rather than reactive."*

— Jim Atkinson, Executive Vice President,
Key Bank Corporation

*"There are two things, in my judgment, it takes to be a **Great Employee**. First, a commitment to the organization and its goals. Second, a balance between work, recreation, family, friends and a continuing desire to grow in knowledge."*

— Fred H. Burrow, President, Burrow Consulting Services

*"**Great Employees** are constantly thinking about the customer. He or she is always looking for ways to improve the product or service for the customer."*

— Gary Ames, President and CEO, USWest Communications

*"A **Great Employee** is one who shares a sense of ownership in the business (profit-sharing helps)—one who takes pride in knowing the business inside and out, and is loyal to his or her employer."*

— Captain Gerald L Coffee, U.S. Navy (Ret.), POW for seven years; presently Author and Speaker

*"**Great Employees** understand that we are nowhere without happy, satisfied 'customers' who will return."*

— Norm Daniels, CEO, G.I Joe's, dated 1995

*"A **Great Employee** knows that a sale is never really made until the customer comes back a second time."*

— Morris Israel, CTR Business Systerms, dated 1913

*"A **Great Employee** figures out how to add value to the work group and the company—and adds it—and lets it be known."*

— Barbara Karmel,Ph.D., President of The Reed Company; Director of U.S. National Bank; Member of The American Psychological Association; and Member of The National Academy of Mangement

"There must be lights burning brighter somewhere, got to be birds flying in higher in a sky more blue."
— Elvis

9
If I Can Dream—Elvis!

A s an old rock-and-roll buff, I had to get Elvis into my book somewhere. Besides that, all the books written about the King have been a success. But there is obviously more to it than that. Elvis started as a kid with a dream and he did everything possible to pursue that dream. And in doing so, he led the change in the complexion of popular music. Much like Craig McCaw changed the form and use of telephones, or Bill Gates changed the use and impact of personal computers.

These people probably wouldn't qualify as **Great Employees,** but they did make great contributions to their fields of endeavor. And all had to overcome huge obstacles to succeed. The odds of their success were minuscule; but they conquered their fears, they used their imagination, they forced their dreams to challenge their minds. They forced every ounce of energy into their dreams—and they succeeded. Dreaming is the seed for success.

Stop for a moment and dream. Put your imagination into it. Close your eyes. If you are a skier, think of helicopter skiing if you have never done it. Try to imagine the sound of the chopper's blades. Smell the fuel, feel the cold. You are about to be dropped onto the snow. Your heart starts pounding. Feel the excitement. You are about to pop into your skis. You have been waiting for this moment since you began skiing. Now it has arrived. Wait, how could it arrive? It's just a dream.

The wonderful thing about dreams is that you can go anywhere; you can do anything. There is one word that doesn't exist in dreams—the word cannot. No one can stop you in a dream. Dreams can make you happy and laugh. Dreams can make you sad and cry. It's all up to you.

The first dream I can remember was when I was four years old. My dream was to become a cowboy. My heroes were Hopalong Cassidy and Roy Rogers. I had an imaginary horse named Trigger. From there, I remember dreaming I had a "nice home and family." Mine were pretty crummy. I guess that is why I dreamt so much—to escape the reality of an unhappy family situation. Well, it is about time to give you the last *Great Employees'* definition.

The *Great Employees'* Definition of a Dream: The One Thought That Seems Impossible, But Is Not.

The mind is still the most powerful machine known to man. The computer cannot yet dream. It will someday, but until then we must rely on our own set of dreams. Look around for a moment. Everything you see was once someone's dream. Even if you are in the middle of a forest with no sign of mankind, Someone had a dream to create that forest.

We talked about priorities and goals in Chapter 2. It is important to recognize the difference between priorities and a dream. From the **Great Employees'** definition you can see that a dream is different. A dream may not be one of your priorities and if so, it has no goals. A dream is so far out there that it may seem impossible at the present time.

But, if a dream is truly a dream it will recur in your thoughts, and at some point in your life, that dream will become a passion. When it does, you will have a new priority. That new priority just might change your life forever, to bring you a new-found excitement with life. Think of a time when you were really enthusiastic about something. The pursuit of a dream will make you a hundred times more excited.

Not all of your dreams will become priorities or goals. And that's okay. Just chasing your dreams can give you a rush. If all of my dreams were to become priorities and I had to accomplish all of the goals to achieve them, I would have to live forever. In fact, that is one of my dreams.

Ten years ago, writing this book was a dream. It had not become a priority. It was too far out there. My dream was to write a book to help other employees cope with a variety of job challenges. The dream was to write this terrific book that would become a best seller. I would travel the country lecturing and selling my book. It would make me semi-famous. And for that I would be handsomely rewarded.

Pursuing a dream usually requires that you make some change, and change can be very scary. Most of us follow the path of least resistance throughout our lives. As hard as most of us work, that is hard to believe. However, when you follow the path of least resistance, you get to stay in your comfort zone. You don't feel challenged.

If you want to remove yourself from that comfort zone you might want to read a great book titled, *DO IT! Let's Get Off Our Buts,* written by Peter McWilliams. His book helped me to muster the courage to abandon my comfort zone and make my dream my priority.

For a dream to become a priority there must first be a commitment. To set out to conquer a dream may take personal sacrifice far beyond anything you have yet to experience. But it may not seem that way because you will be so immersed in pursuing your dream. The pursuit will bring you much happiness and success.

I like the secret to happiness found in the movie, *City Slicker.* When Billy Crystal asks Jack Palance what the secret to happiness is, Palance points with one finger and says, "Just one thing." Although he doesn't say it, that one thing is obviously to live your life by doing whatever makes you happy. That's also the secret to success.

Dreams provide you with an endless source of opportunities. The key to taking advantage of a dream is to, like Peter McWilliams says, "***Do it!***" That's what makes a dream a reality. It seems so simple, but if you have ever committed yourself to pursue a dream, you know it is not. Therefore, let's launch into the **Great Employees' 10 Tips for**:

MAKING DREAMS COME TRUE

1. *You Gotta Have Dreams.* So let's first unleash the most creative source in the world—your mind! Remember, anything can happen in a dream. There are no rules in dreams. The words *can't* and *if* are not found in dreams. Keep that creative spirit flowing.

2. *Cultivate Some Dreams.* Become more conscious of your thoughts. Listen to yourself. Remember, your dreams are private property if you choose. That means you can do whatever you want, whenever you want, in a dream. Anything. So be creative and positive with this ability. Now go for it. What have you always wanted to do? Whom do you envy because of their job or status? Where have you always wanted to go? Where would you be five years from now if there was nothing to get in your way?

3. ***Interpret Your Dreams. Great Employees*** have taken the extra time to interpret their dreams. That means they have thought about the purpose behind their dreams. They ask themselves, "How many times have I had this dream?" They realize that a dream can transform itself into a priority. At that point their dream is on its way to becoming a reality.

4. ***Dreams Can be Fantasies.*** A good friend of mine, who is quite humorous, said his dream was to be with Christy Brinkley on a deserted island. This guy is shorter and funnier that Danny DeVito. So, don't hesitate. Find some fun in those recreational dreams.

5. ***Time to Do Something,*** But what? All right, a dream has been gnawing at you for quite some time. Maybe a year, maybe three. If so, it's time to do something about it. You may want to make it a priority, or decide to continue to dream. There will come a point where you decide to do something, even quit dreaming. But usually your subconscious will take care of that for you. But let's say you decide this dream is telling you, "Here I am, do something with me." What do you do? Read on.

6. ***The Road to Reality.*** The roads that take dreams to reality are many. Lots of dreams become reality because of sheer luck. Some dreams become reality through hard work.

For years I dreamed about writing this book. In recent years, I found myself in bookstores looking for a book similar to this one. I found myself trying to find information on how to write and publish a book. I began talking about it more. The dream became more intense until it took over. At that point I knew I must get on with it.

7. ***You Are Reality.*** We are now to the point of taking this dream seriously. We now know that it is on its way to becoming a reality. There is only one way for it to happen— you. This is your baby. You must take 100% responsibility for your dream, which is now a life priority. As I said earlier, it really takes guts to follow your dream. To make a dream become a reality we are talking mega-commitment.

8.   ***Reality Takes Writing.*** You are now to the point where you must start writing things down. You must build that road to reality. You will have a period where accomplishing the dream is just too complicated. It will be overwhelming. Do not quit. Remember, this dream has been long in the making. Just keep writing down ideas about the dream. Anything that comes to mind write down. It may be just a couple of words. Just keep thinking (dreaming) and writing.

9.   ***Dreams Become Priorities.*** First, write out the dream. Second write out the goals which will have to be accomplished to achieve the dream. At that instant, your dream has become a priority. Third, plan the strategies to accomplish the goals to accomplish your dream (now a priority). And remember to build a time line. Let's try one:

PRIORITY: Buy a new Corvette by July, 1996.

GOAL: Sell gun collection by December, 1995.

STRATEGIES: Advertise in Gun Collectors Weekly: Cost $300.

Sell guns at Sports and Gun Show in August.

Consign antique rifles to Jackson's Gun Store.

GOAL: Buy three cars to refurbish and sell by June of 1996.

STRATEGIES: Refinance existing car to buy a 1990 Mustang.

Buy a 1990 Mustang Convertible to detail and sell by July, 1995.

Use that money to buy 1990 Jeep by October to sell during snow season, February, 1996.

Use that money to buy 1993 Corvette to detail and sell by June 1996.

You may have additional goals and strategies to generate the money for the new Corvette. Please refer to Chapter 2. The challenge is to get started. But you can do it. I know you can.

10.

Become a Great Employee. You are an intelligent and capable person. You have the ability to do anything that is important enough to you. You may lack the confidence or courage to go for the home run. Dream on. The desire will create the confidence. The need will create the courage. If your dream is to be a *Great Employee*, my hat is off to you. When you feel you have become a *Great Employee*, drop me a line or give me a call. I would love to hear from you. And I sincerely hope this little book helped you along the way. Good luck, and follow your dreams.

"Ever seen a blind man cross the road tryin' to get to the other side?"

— Rod Stewart

10

Challenge— You Got What It Takes?

A t this point, you have been provided with hundreds of years of experience condensed into the previous ninety pages. You have been exposed to eight definitions of important traits you must develop to become a *Great Employee*. In each chapter, you have been given *10 Tips* to help you become a *Great Employee*. And you have been exposed to thirty six quotes, from some pretty outstanding people, to help you understand what it takes to be a *Great Employee*.

At this point, it is up to you! We talked about that earlier in the chapter on attitude. Actually, we have touched on it in all of the chapters. At this point, only you can decide if you want to become a *Great Employee*. If you don't, that's okay. There are lots of employees out there who really don't want to put in the time and effort to achieve greatness.

For those of you who read the book and don't aspire to become a *Great Employee*, I hope you have picked up a few pieces of information to help your on you way. For those of you who are already *Great Employees*, I am sure you will use this book to further improve your performance. And, for those of you who are average employees and want to improve and become *Great Employees*, here is your ticket to success. But you have to use the book. Take it to work. Refer to it for little reminders or nudges.

Now, I am not going to leave you high and dry, by saying, "It's all in the book." No way. In this chapter, as in all the others, we are going to talk about some real life experiences, some of which are very moving. And, we will finish up with our *Great Employees' 10 Tips for Accepting the Challenge*. So with that, let's go to the last definition.

The *Great Employees'* Definition of Challenge: Not Accepting the Path of Least Resistance.

As we travel our course through life, we will be faced with many challenges. We are confronted with many obstacles which require hard work, perseverance, sacrifice, and commitment.

Too often the magnitude of the opportunity seems so enormous that we make the decision not to accept the challenge. At that point, we move on to another opportunity which does not require the same extreme challenge for accomplishment. We say to ourselves, "That priority or goal is more me." That is called following the path of least resistance.

We have all accomplished a goal, project, or job that we thought might be impossible at the onset. Take a minute and try to recall one of those instances. It will probably take some time to come up with one, but think hard. What was it like? How did you feel? What did it take to accomplish the task?

I think I can tell you how it felt. There was a positive feeling of pride. You felt happiness. You may have felt euphoric. It was probably one of those times when you said to yourself (out loud), "Yes!" You also probably wanted to find someone to tell about your accomplishment—not bragging, just enthusiastic and excited.

There is a pattern that exists when you accomplish a difficult task. And many of the elements found within that pattern are contained in this book. So, if you choose to accept my challenge, read on. And please bear in mind, each of you can become a *Great Employee* if you choose to make it your priority.

The chapter name asks, "Do you have what it takes?" Because reading about *Great Employees* and making that decision to become one are two very different endeavors, that commitment should not be made lightly. It means sacrifice. I thought it might help if I related to you some stories about people who I have known who have overcome huge obstacles and made their dreams their challenges.

Joe Ivko. Joe has a special place in my heart as he is my father-in-law. In 1966 he was 40. He worked for the Northern Indiana Public Service Company. He had recently made the decision to return to being a lineman after being a foreman, so he would have more time to spend with his children. He and his wife were expecting their seventh child.

Joe was sent to dismantle some high-power equipment that was supposed to have been de-energized. It wasn't and Joe was hit by 7,200 volts of electricity which burned his arms so badly that they had to be amputated above the elbow.

Now, you know that a lot of people would give up, sue, and lay blame on their employer. Not Joe. He made the best of it and he began his search for independence. He has become an inventor, and he and his wife own a manufacturing company.

Joe found that the prosthetic arms were not adequate. So he invented the RIMJET bearing, which allowed him to drive a car, shave, and open heavy doors. I witnessed him ride alone and steer a sled down a mountain with a 2000 foot vertical drop.

After the bearing, he later realigned the cable on the arms to give them longer life. Prosthetic arms now use both his inventions. He did not stop there. He has also invented an apparatus that allows someone with no arms to put on their pants without assistance. And, he has invented a bidet that sells for about $100. If you have priced bidets lately (you probably haven't), they go for over $2500.

Joe is now 70 and is close to being independent. But that isn't enough. He is still inventing and manufacturing.

Bob Wieland. If you ever met Bob, you would never forget him. Bob is full of enthusiasm and personal strength. In high school, he was a star baseball pitcher. Then came the Vietnam War. Bob had a just few days left on his "tour" when he stepped on a field mine.

The result of that last step was the loss of both legs. Now, you probably have seen Vietnam veterans in wheel chairs. Some have gone on to be very successful and some have faced lives of hardship.

But I believe I am accurate when I say that Bob is the only double amputee who has run the Boston Marathon on his hands. He actually uses his hands with small attachments to raise his body higher that the ground. He moves his arms forward and then swings his body forward and lands on what is left of his legs. Bob has also completed the Iron Man Triathlon in Hawaii. It took him 28 days, but he did it.

Bob was a speaking at a meeting I had organized. Bob sometimes gets around in a wheelchair. Not taking care of details, I did not furnish a runway for him. About thirty minutes before his presentation, I realized my error. I said, "Bob, I am sorry there is no runway for the stage. I will help you up." He responded, "Don't worry. I'll make it."

When it was his time to speak, he moved his wheel chair down the aisle to the stage. Once there, he jumped out of the chair, folded it together, with one arm picked it up and lifted it above his head onto the stage. By this time, the audience of 500 was astounded. Then Bob reached up and lifted himself onto the stage, unfolded his wheelchair, lifted himself into the chair and began speaking. By the end of his speech there was not a dry eye in the house.

After that speech he started a "run" across the United States. I haven't talked to him since he began the run, but I know he completed it. There is no doubt in my mind.

Okay, so now you know what is possible when people set their minds to it. But you also need to know that these people do not think they have done anything out of the ordinary. They have taken what they have and made the best out of it. They knew the challenge would be enormous. They knew the obstacles would be many. But they also knew they were not going to accept the path of least resistance. They were going to do what they set out to do.

These people are made of the same thing as you and me. They have taken control of their lives rather than letting their conditions taking control of them. And you must understand that, given the same circumstances, you could do the same thing. But you are not being asked to do the same thing. You are being asked to accept my challenge to become a *Great Employee.* Will this challenge have the dramatic impact on your life as it did for my friends? Maybe not. But then again, maybe it will.

Let's identify the *Great Employees' 10 Tips On:*

Accepting the Challenge

1. *Make the decision to take charge of your life.* This is so important. But you know something, most of us don't have control of our lives. For most of us, our jobs, our families, or our surroundings control us. To get hold of your life and control it, you are going to have to follow many of the *Great Employees' 10 Tips* from Chapters 1, 2, 3, and 9. You can't do it all, but use some of the tips to get on top of things.

2. *Focus on what you have and disregard what you don't.* Let's not belabor this one. When I was six years old and dirt poor, my mom told me, "I cried because I had no shoes, until I met a man with no feet."

3. *Recognize that you must pay a price for the cost of success.* Like it or not, the world is competitive. To succeed you must be willing to work harder than the next person. We are talking capitalism here, not socialism or communism. I hope you like capitalism.

4. *Do not accept average. Great Employees* are not average employees. Larry Wilson, Chairman of the Pecos River Learning Clinics told me a story that goes like this. A person starts a new job and his or her performance is rated at a 10. Pretty soon that person learns that it only takes a 6 to get by on the job. Soon that person is performing at a level 6. I have seen that happen so many times it hurts. Don't fall into that trap.

5. *Practice accepting challenges.* Start with small challenges and graduate to bigger challenges. You gotta walk before you run. Joe Ivko did not put on his new arms and drive a car. It took him years before he could drive himself without the aid of a companion. And now, with his "arms," he can drive alone.

6. *Recognize that to become Great at anything you must be overcome with the dedication and drive.* "Average" takes a little work. "Better than average" takes more work. "Super" takes a lot of work. "Great" takes devotion, dedication, and drive.

7. ***Keep telling yourself you are a great person and build confidence in yourself.*** I keep telling you to do this so you will keep doing it. Nothing will help you be you more than confidence. If somebody gives you a compliment, grab it and savor it.

8. ***Accept setbacks.*** I love setbacks. They push you that much harder. You learn more from one setback than one hundred successes. Remember that!

9. ***Never, never lose sight of your dream, your priority, or your goal.*** Take inventory once in awhile. We talked about that in Chapters 2, 3, 6 and 7. Revisit those chapters from time to time.

10. ***Celebrate success.*** Whatever you do, do me one favor. When you accomplish something you feel is worth of a pat on the back, be sure to pat yourself on the back. If you do it, nobody else needs to do it.

11. And since this is the last chapter, I get to enjoy some author's freedom. If, for any reason, you would like to call me to discuss a challenge or problem you have at work, feel free to do so. You will always have a willing listener. Just remember I am on Pacific Time. The telephone number is 503-697-7707.

P.S. Work on those dreams and challenges. There will come a time in your life, when dreams and challenges will be replaced by memories.

GOOD LUCK TO YOU AND YOUR CAREER!

Walt Mulvey is available for keynote speeches, workshops and seminars. He can be reached at 503-697-7707.

ORDER FORM

Qty.	Title	Price	Can.Price	Total
	Winning at Work	$10.00	$13.00	
			Subtotal	
	Shipping and Handling (add $3.00 for one book, $2.00 for each additional book)			
	Sales tax (WA residents only, add 8.2%)			
			Total Enclosed	

Telephone Orders:
Call 1-800-468-1994.
Have your VISA or
Mastercard ready.

FAX Orders:
1-206-672-8597. Fill out
order blank and fax.

Postal Orders:
Hara Publishing
P.O. Box 19732
Seattle, WA 98109

Payment: Please Check One:

☐ Check

☐ VISA

☐ MasterCard

Expiration Date: _____ / _____
Card #: _____
Name on Card: _____

NAME _____

ADDRESS _____

CITY _____ STATE _____ ZIP _____

DAYTIME PHONE _____

Quantity discounts are available.
For more information, call 503-697-7707.
Thank you for your order!
I understand that I may return any books for a full refund if not satisfied.